Reflections!!!
A Faith Based Journey in Poetry

Francisco J. Torres

Reflections!!!
A Faith-Based Journey in Poetry
Copyright © 2023 by Francisco J. Torres

ISBN-13: Paperback: 978-1-64749-890-0
         Hardback: 978-1-64749-891-7
         ePub: 978-1-64749-892-4

All rights reserved. No part of this publication may be reproduced, distributed, or transmitted in any form or by any means, including photocopying, recording, or other electronic or mechanical methods, without the prior written permission of the publisher or author, except in the case of brief quotations embodied in critical reviews and certain other noncommercial uses permitted by copyright law.

Although every precaution has been taken to verify the accuracy of the information contained herein, the author and publisher assume no responsibility for any errors or omissions. No liability is assumed for damages that may result from the use of information contained within.

Printed in the United States of America

GoToPublish LLC
1-888-337-1724
www.gotopublish.com
info@gotopublish.com

FORWARD

The year was 1993, a year in which my plate was so full that something had to give, and that something was me. It was the year that found me deeply immersed in contract negotiations with my union, AFSCME, and the Commonwealth of Pennsylvania, within the Department of the Auditor General, a year in which my wife was pregnant with our second child and resented my involvement with the union since it kept me away at times from the family, a year in which my father now 88 years old, had a heart attack and was near death, and a year that still demanded my being a husband to my wife and a father to my three year old daughter, all the while being a supervisor to auditors assigned to me, while I still had the responsibility of completing my own audits. The result, a nervous breakdown. It was a time, and for many years thereafter, when I was being helped by all who loved me, a time when I was involuntarily committed in and out of the hospital more times than I can remember, and a time when my friends and colleagues, alike, were concerned for me. Yet, nothing seemed to help me overcome my depression and I felt totally alone and abandoned, even by the One Whom I held my most dear, my God. This book is dedicated to the Holy Spirit who lifted me up from my misery, slow but surely, and inspired me to write these poems, over the course of 20 years, as a means of therapy, if you will, and who enabled me to live once again and have hope!!! A faith-based journey being guided by the Holy Spirit, which continues to this very day!!!

It's Not Important To Be Successful,
It's Important To Be Faithful !!!

Mother Teresa

HAVE FAITH IN YOUR FAITH !!!

THERE ARE TIMES IN YOUR LIFE THAT
YOU FEEL LIKE JUST CHUCKING IT ALL,
YOU CAN'T TAKE IT ANYMORE, YOU FEEL OVERWHELMED
AND YOU'RE WILLING TO TAKE THAT LONG DEEP FALL;

YOU'RE SO FULL OF DOUBTS, CONFUSED AND DISHEARTENED
AND WONDER IF ANY OF THIS MAKES SENSE,
YOU'RE DISGUSTED, FRUSTRATED AND FEEL SO TOTALLY ALONE
THAT YOU'RE WILLING TO GIVE IT ALL AWAY FOR AS
LITTLE AS SIX PENCE;

YET, IT'S AT THESE PRECISE MOMENTS THAT
GOD'S GIFT OF FAITH KICKS IN,
AND YOUR FAITH TELLS YOU THAT YOUR BURDEN WILL NEVER
BE MORE THAN YOU CAN BEAR AND THAT YOU CAN WIN;

BECAUSE GOD ISN'T FINISHED WITH YOU UNTIL YOU DRINK
FROM HIS SON'S CUP OF WINE,
SO, YOU MUST COOPERATE AND ACCEPT HIS GIFTS OF GRACE
THAT HELP YOU STAND THE TEST OF TIME AND RUN ACROSS
THAT FINISH LINE;

SO, DON'T GIVE UP, DON'T QUIT, AND BY ALL MEANS, DON'T THROW YOUR FAITH AND LIFE AWAY, HAVE FAITH IN YOUR FAITH, FOR GOD HAS PLANS FOR YOU IN HIS MANSION, AND HE ONLY WISHES TO REFINE AND MOLD YOU, FOR HE IS THE POTTER AND YOU ARE THE CLAY !!!

YODA !!!
7-10-2003

I LOVE YOU!!!

How does one say thank you to someone Who has never forsaken nor has
                                                                                Failed you,
I suppose you can sing His praises, talk about His mighty deeds, or shout for
                                                                              Joy till you turn blue.

Beautiful lyrics from the song "Lady"* would also seem so appropriate in
    praising our Lord, as Kenny Rogers sang, "I'm your knight in shining
                Armor...you made me what I am, and I am yours",
Yet, it hardly seems enough in saying thanks to someone Who has
  Overlooked my many faults, Who has forgiven me countless times, and
    Who has graciously healed me and made me whole, with His multitude
                                                                                      Of cures.

How can One so Awesome, so Powerful and filled with Wisdom even give me
                                                   The time of day or glance my way,
Yet He faithfully shows me and lovingly reassures me that I am worth it, as we
  Both reflect on the day His hands created me and how He has molded me as
                                                        I aged, like a child at play.

I suppose it would take a lifetime looking for the perfect gift, the eloquent
  Words, the soothing melody or the loving gesture to say, "THANK YOU", for
                                                                    All that YOU have done,
But I know of no better way to express my profound heartfelt " THANKS",
  Other than the way He gently whispers in my ear, " I LOVE YOU",
                                                                           to "HIS SON!!!"

                                                                          YODA!!!
                                                                         9-4-2003

*Song: "Lady"
Released in 1977
Artist: Kenny Rogers

Lord, do not let my weakness
And failures overwhelm me. Give me the faith
And hope I need to begin again each day
To be your faithful disciple.

(An excerpt from a church bulletin)

WHY !!!

What is it about man's nature that we can't accept the Lord's way and always have to rebel and question Him by asking the infamous question "Why ?",

We act like children that didn't get his or her own way and so in frustration and anger we sit down, pout and cry;

As we grow older and move into our teens, we begin to think we know it all and have all the answers, so there is no reason anymore to ask "Why?",

So, we go through life making excuses for ourselves when things don't turn out right, or quick to blame others, or worse, begin to lie;

When we reach young adulthood and make our break from home, it's not long till that infamous question begins to haunt us and we again cry out "Why ?",

As it becomes increasingly difficult to find a job, to fall in love, to make new friends or to deal with people who can't be trusted or are sly;

Even when we become financially secure, or become influential and powerful, or meet that someone special in our lives who makes us feel like we're on cloud nine, we feel we have no need anymore to ask "Why ?",

Yet, for some, it's not always roses and things quickly sour and before you know it, fortunes are lost, we are quickly humbled and the vows we have made become meaningless and someone is saying bye;

And as we age, and loved ones and friends alike begin to fade away, that cry in the wilderness becomes more pronounced as we scream out in anguish, grief and sorrow and demand to know "Why ?",

Yet, God has remained faithful and has seen us through our trials and tribulations and is at our side; guiding us, protecting us and comforting us, as we sigh;

Because, you see, it doesn't matter to Him how many times we have failed, lost our way or abandoned and blamed Him as we asked "Why ?",

For, all He wants from us is to Love Him, accept His Son as our Saviour and allow ourselves to be guided by the Holy Spirit as we repent and live out our lives by trying to practice our gift of faith before we die;

So, the next time you feel the need to blame, abandon or question our Lord by asking "Why ?",

Ask yourself this question, "Did I even make an honest effort to practice my Faith, Love my God and accept His ways, or am I simply refusing to try !!!"

YODA !!!
12-22-03

REACHING OUT!!!

O my God, the beautiful ways and names that there are to describe you, some given by You, O Lord, and others by man himself; Lord, Master, God, Creator, Emmanuel, Saviour, Messiah, Redeemer, Word Incarnate, King, Teacher, Raboni, Wonderful, Counselor, Paraclete, Mediator, Rabbi, Missionary, Good Shepherd, Father, Yahweh, I Am; all calling and reaching out to You, O Lord, my God and Saviour;

Yet, this is only a small litany of Judeo/Christian names given to our God to describe Him, and we as Christians, are only a small fraction of all of God's children that live on this earth, leaving me to wonder, what else is our Heavenly Father known as or called, and how He is experienced by His other children, within their hearts, minds and souls, as they too seek out their Creator and attempt to describe and communicate with Him through their sight, sound, touch, words and flavour.

Surely, God in His infinite Wisdom and Love cherishes and inspires all His children to seek Him out and find Him within all His creation, whether that be within our fellow man, nature or creature, placed upon this earth that He has created, blesses and looks upon with paternal Love;

And, if one observes very closely, one can see evidence of that search and presence of our God in examples such as in beautiful lyrics of songs sung and soothing melodies of music played in praise of our Lord, or the smile of a new born infant gazing into your eyes and touching the very depths of your soul, or the beauty of winter's gentle falling snow white blanket covering and tucking in God's sleepy earth, or the artist's or sculptor's inspiration, interpretation and capture of the Holy Spirit painted on canvas or chiseled in marble, depicted as a Dove.

And, as we begin to search, discover, understand, share, embrace and Love our God and one another, we begin to see and experience the commonality within each other as God's children, as well as the magnificence, beauty and awesomeness of our Lord;

However, we still have such a long way to go on this pilgrimage, even in this 21st century of ours, because we are still plagued by the prejudice, injustice, arrogance, self-serving interests, oppressiveness, greed and hatred that we continue to practice and treat one another because of our differences in race, creed, color, gender and/or nationality, as if we are doomed to this fate and can't escape its vicious cycle because we are bound and imprisoned by our own weaknesses and sins, as if tied to these faults by cord.

As we attempt to break free from our bondage and reach out to others, there are some who are quick to raise the flag of caution or shout the "call to arms", who point out that non-Christian ways are pagan ways, or who adamantly state that Christianity is the only faith that possesses the truth and the way, as ministers, pastors and priests threaten damnation from the pulpit if you stray;

It's as if we think we have a lock on God, whose existence is solely for our own benefit, it's as if we view and treat our Lord in the same manner that capitalism conducts its business by striving to create a monopoly or to corner the market on the Creator, or how we as Christians have adopted the American way as it is arrogantly promulgated to the rest of the world, by presenting ourselves as the chosen ones and the only one who can play.

Naively, all that we are doing when we behave in this manner is to show our own self-centeredness, insecurities, prejudices, ignorance, immaturity, self-righteousness and lack of faith in our own faith, as we are quick to zero in on and point out the differences that separate us rather than concentrate on what we have in common and can mutually share;

We don't have to look far for examples of that commonality, when right here in America, in their own backyard as opposed to our backyard, we have the American Indian culture and it's portrayal of the Creator as the "Great Spirit", Who also inspires His children in prayer whom utter such beautiful words as, "…I seek strength, not to be greater than my brother, but to fight my greatest enemy—myself. Make me always ready to come to you with clean hands and straight eyes. So when life fades as the fading sunset, my spirit may come to you without shame"*, surely, this is the same God that I love and wish to seek out, in such a similar and beautiful manner, and can only dream that someday, I too, can also pray to our Lord with such eloquence as prayed by this Indian whose heart and soul has been laid bare and given as a gift to his creator, in reverent words that care .

Are we, as modern day Christians, when we encounter and deal with one another, any different than the scribes, Sadducees and Pharisees in Christ's time who meticulously and scrupulously followed "the letter of the law" but failed to comprehend, embrace and practice "the spirit of the law", as in the lesson taught from Scripture when Christ was confronted by His enemies and had the adulteress, Mary Magdalene, presented before Him to judge the sin she bore?

Many lessons can be learned from this passage of Scripture as we study it, for we can see the Wisdom, Compassion, Justice, Power, Authority, Mercy and Love of Christ, in action, as He symbolically transforms the sin of the adulteress into a mirror that reflects, exposes and weighs the sins of all who gaze upon her and suddenly, no one is able to bear the sight, shame and burden of their own sins, caught in their own trap, as all drop their heavy stones of sin and leave the scene, one by one, leaving Christ alone with the woman, prompting Christ to ask the woman,"…where are they? Has no one condemned you? She replied, 'No one, Sir.' Then Jesus said Neither do I condemn you…", unveiling His Wisdom and Compassion by demonstrating that God's ways are not our ways, giving us a new insight and comprehension of His Justice and as Author of these laws, how even the laws are subject to His Power and Authority, and unfolds before the woman, for her to intuitively recognize, understand and accept that she was chosen as God's instrument to reveal the beauty, magnificence and righteousness of His Mercy and Love as she is the only one left standing before Christ, because He has not judged her sin, as the others have judged their own sins and have condemned themselves, and if she desires to remain in God's presence and grace, then she must listen to Christ's final words of closure as to what has just happened, "Go, and from now on do not sin anymore."

It was once said, "As you live for today, look to the past, for in it lies your future", implying that if we don't learn from the lessons of the past as Divinely written in the Bible, are we doomed too, to make the same mistakes today and likewise be damned forever in eternity, unworthy to bare the name of the God that we profess to worship and love, and instead, continue to shout our war cry, rally to the "call to arms" and defiantly rattle our saber;

Or, can we someday truly experience "the promises of Christ", by breaking free from our sins of bondage and be made worthy to bear the name of Christian, Child of God, Peacemaker, and Brother, by reaching out and embracing all of God's children, freely and unconditionally, whether Jewish, Christian, Muslim, Hindu, Buddhist; black, white, red, yellow; man, woman; Russian, American, Arab, Jew; etc., and foremost by obeying and living out the "new commandment" that Christ Himself gave us, which summarizes all of God's commandments, precepts, ordinances, laws, decrees and statutes, into one simple commandment for all to understand and obey, "Love God and Love Your Neighbor!!!

YODA!!!
9-9-2004

*"An Indian Prayer"
Red Cloud Indian School
Pine Ridge
South Dakota

CRUSHED !!!

Turn your head and back and pretend that you
                             Don't see what I am about to do,
To your friend and neighbor who deserve what they get
                             Because they don't look like me or you;

Who cares, the world is better off
                           With one less black, fetus, Christian or Jew,
After all, their slaves, nothing but tissue, self-righteous
                     Nor really chosen by the One who created we two.

                 And I was crushed by Satan and man and
                                Made to feel low,
         Just because my God gave me the
                               Courage to say NO;

                 But my Lord touched my very soul
                                And lifted me up,
         As I drank from a Chalice that was
                                His Son's Golden Cup !!!

But as always, he never gives up and returns
                          To haunt me with his hatred, sins and lies,
He makes me watch as he inflicts his genocide, abortions,
             Persecutions and anti-Semitism on man hoping that I'll
                        Ignore the pain and agony, as I hear their cries;

For he is relentless and pursues me to no end
                          Because he knows his days are numbered,
As he seeks to destroy the Children of God
        If they don't worship him and thus become encumbered.

        And I was crushed by Satan and man and
                              Made to feel low,
    Just because my God gave me the
                            Courage to say NO;

    But my Lord touched my very soul
                            And lifted me up,
    As I drank from a Chalice that was
                      His Son's Golden Cup !!!

He laughs at me and calls me a fool as I
              Practice my faith and look to my Lord to be saved,
And he tells me it's useless and the road to hell is full of
    Good intentions that are chewed-up, crushed and used like
                            Macadam being paved;

Why waste your time, your efforts and give your Love to someone
        Whom you can't see, nor even talks to you and doesn't need,
Come follow me, and I'll give you the world and all that you want;
    Fulfillment in power, authority, hatred, lies and human greed.

        And I was crushed by Satan and man and
                              Made to feel low,
    Just because my God gave me the
                            Courage to say NO;

But my Lord touched my very soul
                                          And lifted me up,
As I drank from a Chalice that was
                                          His Son's Golden Cup !!!

And so, the story of Good vs. Evil goes on as it did since
                                          The beginning of time,
Knowing that man will continue to fall and get burnt
                                          Like someone carelessly gardening with lime;

But every gardener knows that lime eventually
                                          Sweetens and prepares the soil,
So, we need only to wait, till our Lord comes to save us,
                                          As we practice our Faith and continue to toil.

And I was crushed by Satan and man and
                                          Made to feel low,
Just because my God gave me the
                                          Courage to say NO;

But my Lord touched my very soul
                                          And lifted me up,
As I drank from a Chalice that was
                                          His Son's Golden Cup !!!

YODA !!!
3-26-2005

LONELINESS !!!

Who can ever say that he or she has never felt
                     The sting and agony of feeling alone,

For the trials and tribulations of life have tested us all,
         Causing one's spirit to scream out in emotions of
                 Loneliness, anguish and sorrow, which at
                       Times, can harden one's heart to stone;

No disease, illness, catastrophe, pain, death or evil is more
         Intense or torturing than the sorrow of feeling totally
               Alone, lost, abandoned, orphaned or betrayed,

And even though these sufferings, in and of themselves,
     Are moments that can be overwhelming, they are just
         Precursors leading to the desolation of the heart
            And soul mired in despair and hopelessness, as
                       They practice their trade;

As we attempt to set ourselves free by toiling our way
        Through and suppressing these fiery feelings that
               Consume us, it doesn't take much to
                      Rekindle the emotion,

A gaze upon a scene or picture resurrecting the buried
   Image of a loved one, the taste of delicacies reminding
      Us how we savored the sweetness of a kiss, the melody
          Of a song giving rise and sound to hidden and silent
              Memories , the touch of a hand making us yearn for

The gentleness and warmth of forgotten caresses and
    Hugs, or the aroma of a scent lingering in the air
        Like the fragrance of a sweetheart's perfume
            That was bottled and sold as a love potion;

And just when we feel we can't take it anymore and we
    Are willing to succumb to the seductions of loneliness
        And surrender our broken hearts and tormented souls
            To the netherworld, just to end it all,

Our Faith kicks in and our Lord and Saviour reaches out
    And mends our hearts and embraces our souls with His
        Gentleness, Understanding, Compassion, Mercy and
            Love, as He catches us before we take that long
                Deep fall;

For you see, it is Divinely written that no matter how
  Much you despair and lose all hope, if you accept God's
    Only Son and believe in His Word as written in Scripture,
            As though it was chiseled in stone,

Then Christ Himself has promised, that He will be there
        For you in your "darkest hour" and
            "…you will never stand alone !!!"

                    YODA !!!
                    8-18-2005

THE CALL !!!

"Follow me, and let the dead bury their dead",
   a perplexing statement that almost sounds so cruel,
      yet, Christ is calling you and this may be
         your only chance to be a King or a fool !!!

Why would Christ say to a disciple something so harsh
   and uncharacteristic of Whom we think Christ to be?
Unless we again make that age old mistake of defining God
      by our terms rather than His ways as defined by
         the One Who is composed distinctly into Three.

Could it be that we place tradition, culture, possessions
     and our Love for those around us, foremost,
   rather than giving all our heart, mind, soul and strength to
  the One Who is the Bread of Life and known as the Heavenly Host?

Surely, one would be ostracized, ridiculed and judged
  to be shameless, heartless and insane if it appears that
    one has abandoned his family, relatives, friends

       and responsibilities, by today's secular norms.

However, is Christ's call to you any different today than
   it was in Abraham's or Moses' time to serve the Lord
     at His beckoning, even if it means giving up the ones
       you Love most dearly, in order to serve your God
           and partake in His "Crown of Thorns?"

How do we know that by heeding to the call of Christ,
    it may indeed be most beneficial to yourself and
        your Loved ones whom you hold so dear?
You don't, but that call can not be denied, if you believe,
    because His words and voice are so authoritative,
        yet Loving, and all of a sudden or over time,
            it becomes so crystal clear !!!

For to deny and reject His call is not salutary,
  and you may as well be dead like those who need to be buried,
because Christ will move on looking for those who wish
    to serve Him, rather than those who can't be bothered
        or seem to be so hurried.

Who am I to say, "tomorrow,"
    who am I to say, "I'm too busy,"
        who am I to say, "others are counting on me,"
            who am I to say, **"NO."**

"Tomorrow may be taken from me", *
    what is more important than the mission that lies before me,
        who deserves my Love more than the One Who created me,
           and if "i am" a child of the One Who calls Himself "I AM",
              then, I must **"GO !!!"**
                YODA !!!
                2-19-06

*A quote from a prayer
written by Margaret Wildflower
entitled, "Carry Me Through."

THE DAILY WAGE !!!

"Thus, the last will be first, and the first will be last",
          a statement that is so contrary to contemporary beliefs;
yet, Christ often challenged those beliefs and shattered
   our understanding and cast those broken pieces to the wind
               which are forever tossed about like leaves.

To accept the daily wage for services rendered,
            at day's end, and then complain
                 when paid the prevailing rate;
is like accusing one that a contract has been broken
       and the slighted party becomes angry and full of hate.

To expect more than what was agreed upon
           is presumptuous, selfish and nothing but greed;
and to consider generosity that has been extended
         to others as unjust, is like erroneously
                 calling a grape, a weed.

What would you rather have, sitting idle all day
        with no work to do and earning no wage
            from which to buy your daily bread;
or being fortunate enough to be singled out and selected
       to prove your worth and let your light shine, like
           Rudolph did in leading and pulling Santa's sled.

The message that Christ is sending for all to hear
                                        and obey, is all so very clear;
that by placing others first before yourself,
                                is what God truly holds dear.

For you see, as told by Christ, the first will be last,
                                        and the last will be first;
as God roams the Earth looking for and harvesting
                      the cream of the crop, to quench His thirst !!!

                                                      YODA !!!
                                                      2-24-06

SPIRITUAL WARFARE !!!

" **'Praised be the Lord'**, I exclaim,
    and I am safe from my enemies ….",
        "**a battle cry**" of David said with conviction and passion
            rather than one of his many pleas.

It's "**an affirmation of belief**"
    knowing that God is with you,
        "**shielding you**" from all harm as he protects you,
            from your helmet to your shoe.

Christ's Knight sent *"on a mission"*
    "to take on evil" in any form,
        as the forces of darkness gather
            like bees in a swarm.

It's "**Spiritual Warfare**" fought like
    it has never been fought before,
        "**Good vs. Evil**", a no holds bar struggle,
            with no boundaries from shore to shore.

Satan uses his weapons of lies, greed, betrayal,
    lust, anger and hate as a means of *"confusion"*,
        making it impossible at times to *"discern between*
            right and wrong", as they melt together in fusion.

"An enemy so strong and powerful"
　　　　resorting to anything to win,
　　　　　　　knowing that *"his greatest weapon*
　　　　　　　　　is to lead man to sin."

Yet, *"**Christ too has His arsenal of weapons**"*
　　　and has mustered His troops, waiting in reserve,
　　　　　God's Heavenly Angels, the Communion of Saints, and
　　　　　all of God's earthly creation, eager and

　　　　"ready to serve."

A fight to the death, where *"victory"*
　　　is not defined by the one who is left standing,
　　　　　but rather by the one who takes that *"leap of faith"*
　　　　　　　and remains faithful by embracing Christ as
　　　　　　　　　　his landing.

So, remain steadfast *"**with all your Heart, Soul, Mind**
　　***and Strength**"*, as you take a stand and fight to win,
　　　　by following the *"**Ancient Path**"* which is
　　　　　the only way to be victorious over sin.

For *"**Christ's armor**"* of Forgiveness, Mercy, Compassion, Wisdom
　　Understanding, Humility and *"**Love**"* are not to be out done,
　　　because the price for our *"**victory in salvation**"* has already
　　　　been *"**paid for in blood, by God's only Son !!!**"*

　　　　　　　　　　　　　　　　YODA !!!
　　　　　　　　　　　　　　　　3-21-2006

THE RAINBOW!!!

And God said, "I set my bow in the clouds to serve
    as a sign of the covenant between me and the earth";
        a new beginning with *"a promise of everlasting Love"*
            Like a father and mother would make to their child at birth.

A "rainbow" layered with multiple stripes of hues, pastels
        and transparencies, magnificently displayed for all to see;
      As God is reminded by a promise between Himself and all
           Living beings, to destroy no more, but rather, once again,
                Planting the seeds of *"hope"* and the coming of things to be.

Yet, one can't help but ponder about God's
  infinite *"wisdom and love'* and if He hides from us
    other aspects of His covenant, symbol, wonder and sign?
        For, we have come to realize in life that   *"signs"* can take
          On different or multiple meanings, which may not be fully
              Understood or recognized, because we may be blinded

                      by the obvious or by the way they shine.

For example, as the rain dissipates and the rainbow
   begins to fade away as the *"sun"* becomes more prominent;
      could it be that the *"bow"* represents the old covenant being
         replaced by the fulfillment of God's other promise of the

            "messiah" coming and the establishment of a new covenant?

It's almost as if the rain and colors of the bow are drying up and
    fading away by the warmth and brilliance of God's only "***Son***";
        a "***Love***" so strong, selfless and unconditional,
           that can't be matched bar none.

Or, can it be the "***manifestation of God's Love***"
    that he had for Joseph, the "***dreamer of dreams***";
      "***favored by God***", as well as by his own father, Jacob,
        who made his son a "***cloak of many colors***" sewn in seams.

Perhaps, the bow of many colors represent God's
    many "***children***", all made in "***His***" own "***image***";
      or, is characteristic of the many "*creatures*" placed upon
        this earth by the "***Creator***", that are just as colorful
          and majestic, like the peacock fanning its plumage.

And, if you wish to have some "***fun***" with it, like God
    revels in having fun, then be silly and perhaps even bold;
      by creating a fairy tale or myth that prompts the adventurer or
        believer to follow that "***rainbow***" to its end to find a pot of gold.

The analogies and interpretations are "*endless*", like one would
    contemplate, admiring a piece of art work on display in a show;
    yet, as we imagine the possibilities, one conclusion can be drawn
      for sure by all, and that is, we can see the awesomeness, beauty
        and "***Love***" of our Lord, in something as simple as a "***bow!!!***"

YODA!!!
5-07-06

BUTTERFLY O BUTTERFLY!!!

Butterfly O Butterfly, where do thou come from;
   have you been created from someone's heartfelt desire,
      are you a figment of someone's imagination, or have
          you been given life from someone's Love
              and a sample of things to come?

You spread your delicate wings and allow
      the gentle breeze to carry you away
          as you flutter and dance;
     I become breathless as I watch you
        choreograph your rhythmic movements
            that hypnotize my every glance.

Your fragile wings are like fine garments
    made from the purest of silk, sewn in
        beautiful patterns that are so exquisite;
    my imagination runs wild with emotions, as I gaze
      upon your exotic display of majestic colors and
          pictorial symmetry, which are so implicit.

You joyfully and gracefully dance from
     site to site, like a waltz to music
        making it all seem so easy;
      as you beckon and entice me to dance
        with you, as you tango about, as I watch
          with amazement and become somewhat queasy.

Some of the names by which you are called are so
    eloquent and your beauty is so refined and stately;
        like the Monarch Milkweed, the Silver Emperor,
            the Empress Leilia and the King's Hairstreak,
                all denoting royalty.

Butterfly O Butterfly, surely you must
    have come from Heaven above;
        as God stretched out His hand and
            created you from His infinite Love!!!

YODA!
8-01-06

WHERE HAS "HOPE" GONE???

I don't know, as I look at the world today and see the state that man is in, I must ask myself, Where Has "HOPE" Gone???,

    It appears we live each day, reading the newspaper, hearing on the radio and watching on television, how school children are slaughtered, natural disasters killing thousands, terrorists preying on the innocents, and on, and on, and on!!!

It's enough to make one sick and lose all hope and wonder if there is anything that can be done,

    People have seemed to have lost their way, refusing to get involved and think only of themselves and resorting to solve their problems with a gun.

It all seems so overwhelming, feeling all alone, orphaned, abandoned, and betrayed; having no one to come to our aid or rescue,

    Floundering, searching for someone who has the answers to keep us safe, while finding no one who has a clue.

Perhaps we're looking in the wrong places and have forgotten what our country's foundation was built upon and promulgated,

    A belief in faith that would see them through, to withstand assaults by any enemy, in any form, while standing together as one, refusing to be separated.

The pains and sufferings of today are no different than the pains and sufferings that our nation and its people went through in its early days and formation,

People escaping countries that persecuted and maimed, crossing perilous oceans to a new world that may be hostile, risking it all, while praying to their God for their salvation.

Being tested by the whole world that wanted to grab a piece of this New World and all that it has to offer,
> Looking at its wealth of land, resources, opportunity, and its people; while wanting no more than to pillage, steal, enslave, and fill their coffers.

But our founding fathers, with the blessing of their God and its nation's people, took a stand to fight for all they held dear, in blood and tears, and wrote laws that would protect its citizens and nation, patterned after their faith that had seen them through,
> Enabling them to stand as one, to persevere against all odds, evolving and standing tall, while raising their nation's flag of red, white, and blue.

Many lessons and sense of guidance can be learned by looking at our nation's early days and its people,
> By returning to the one foundation on which everything was built upon, and that was gathering to pray to our God, under the church's steeple.

But one can even go back ages, to a time where it all began, where a Child was born on Christmas morn, The BIRTH OF "HOPE",
> So, look for that star, search for our God, pray on bended knee, open your hearts to our Lord, love your neighbor, and who knows, perhaps that's enough to keep us all from sliding down that fiery slippery slope!!!

YODA
12-20-2022

WHAT'S IN A BIRTHDAY???

What's in a Birthday,
    It's hard to say.

Another year older,
    Growing a little bolder!

What's all the fuss about,
    I wish you would cut it out.

Am I getting a little cynic,
    Is it time to visit a clinic?

Did I forget what it was like,
    To get a present like a brand-new bike.

To be young and so full of excitement,
    Wanting it to last as I capture the moment.

Oh, how I wish the candles weren't so many,
    Dreaming like a kid, wanting my presents to be plenty.

But I know things are different now,
    Moving forward, like an ox to a plow.

So, what can I say for myself,
    As I reflect on the past year's untold wealth.

Well, as I pondered and reminisced,
> I could see that my treasures were many, and I felt quite blessed.

Phone calls from brothers, sisters and friends, wishing me well,
> An outpouring of Love, letting me know I'm not forgotten, all making my head swell.

Volunteering to repair homes for people in need,
> Making me forget about myself and any feelings of greed.

Seeing the appreciation, gratitude and smiles on their faces,
> While looking forward to the next project, knowing there are plenty of needy places.

Playing golf with childhood friends and guys and gal from our Wednesday group,

> Full of laughter, banter and comradery; blending together like a well-made pot of soup.

Going to church to worship and give thanks and praise to Yahweh,
> Feeling humble and thankful to receive His Son, as I bow my head and
>> pray.

So, if I seemed a little cynical at first,
> Don't mind me, for I am known for an occasional outburst.

For I know it's not all those accolades, parties, presents and years that count,
> Rather, it's family, friends, neighbors, and the Great I Am, that make me feel like Royalty, like a Count!!!

So, I look forward to the next year and all the blessings that may come my way,
> Dreaming of new adventures, friendships, and Love; feeling like a kid, once more, at play!!!

YODA
12-22-22

TIS THE SEASON
ITS HERE!!! ITS HERE!!! ITS HERE!!!

Finally, its Christmas Eve and all the preparations and dreams of joy, laughter, presents and family gatherings are coming to fruition, making me want to climb to the roof top and shout, "ITS HERE!!!, ITS HERE!!!, ITS HERE!!!"

The day before Christ is born; a day full of anticipation and excitement, trying to calm the kids down as they dream of what Santa may bring, my wife wrapping last minute gifts for family and friends, while I'm exhausted from all the preparations leading up to this Holiday, as I collapse in my red leather lazy-boy, sipping on a bottle of beer.

Slowly, I began to fade away, doing what I do best, taking a nap, while dreaming of all that Christmas brings, knowing full well that all the hard work, money spent, and prayers said to our Lord for peace on earth, are all worth it.

There is no other time on Earth when people come together, to celebrate a day held so dear to everyone's heart, when pain and suffering seems to take a back seat though not forgotten, an excitement so strong and full of hope that can't be contained; like a Knight's battle tested steed hearing the drumbeats, eager for battle, while chomping on its bit.

My nap is now leading me by hand to a place far, far away, where another family gave birth to this very day that we call Christmas; a family so ordinary, yet chosen by God, even though they held no title and whose means were oh so very meager.

It started with a young carpenter named Joseph, wanting the hand of a young girl named Mary, to be his wife, and so the story unfolded, as the two not knowing where their marriage would lead; a life that some might consider to be oh so full of strife, pain and feelings of beleaguer.

Mary, visited by the Archangel Gabriel, who announced to the world that she was chosen by God, to be the mother of His only Son, if only she would say "YES!!!".

She was so afraid and so full of doubts since she did not know man, even though she was told not to be, by the angel Gabriel; as he gently and soothingly reassured her that the Holy Spirit would descend upon her to conceive and give birth, as God would stretch out His Hand upon her and BLESS!!!

Reaching deep within her very soul and heart, she relied on her faith and trusted in the God that she LOVED so dearly by saying, "May it be done to me according to your word." Words enough for the angel Gabriel to hear, that would seal the beginning and fulfill the establishment of the new covenant that was promised, a Messiah that would save God's people, and so, he departed.

As my nap continued to lead me through the Christmas story of hardships, danger and fear that Mary and Joseph would encounter, all the while knowing in hindsight as revealed by Scripture, it was obvious and endearing, that God would not allow His chosen to be without, harmed or outsmarted.

I now saw the "Christmas Star", high above, shining oh so bright, that would lead the world to "THE BIRTH OF HOPE", as I watched three sojourning Magi who were led to give worship on bended knee, to the newborn Babe, wrapped in swaddling clothes and laying in a manager, as they laid their gifts of gold, frankincense, and myrrh, before Him, gifts fit for a King!!!

My head, heart and very being were now filled with emotions of joy, excitement and hopefulness, as I too gazed upon the newborn Babe, much like the wise men and shepherds had surely felt and seen, as we all listened to heavenly songs, commanded by the Father, for HIS angels to sing!!!

Suddenly and abruptly, I was being shaken and awakened by my girls, screaming and shouting, "Daddy, daddy, daddy, is Santa coming, is Santa coming, is Santa coming???", as I slowly opened my sleepy wandering eyes that looked about, while I picked-up my bottle of beer that fell to the floor.

"YES!!!", I said, as I gathered them together and placed them on my lap, reassuring them that they had been good and Santa would not forget them nor abandon them; as I started to tell them about a story that the whole world was waiting for and "WHO" was coming, and how like them, a young girl, chosen by God, would play a part in saving the whole world someday, by the "CHILD" she blessedly would bore!!!

YODA
12-24-2022

www.ingramcontent.com/pod-product-compliance
Lightning Source LLC
LaVergne TN
LVHW041553060526
838200LV00037B/1269